BIG
& LITTLE

Steve Jenkins

Houghton Mifflin Company

Boston 1996

For Page and Alec

For information about this and other Houghton MIfflin trade and reference books and multimedia products, visit The Bookstore at Houghton Mifflin on the World Wide Web at http://www.hmco.com/trade/.

Manufactured in the United States of America

Book design by Steve Jenkins
The text of this book is set in 14-point Palatino.
The illustrations are cut-paper collage, reproduced in full color.

BVG 10 9 8 7 6 5 4 3 2 1

Library of Congress Cataloging-in-Publication Data
Steve Jenkins.
Big and little / by Steve Jenkins
p. cm.
Summary: Illustrates the concept of size by comparing different animals, from the smallest visible animals to the largest.
ISBN 0-395-72664-6
1. Body size — Miscellanea — Juvenile literature.   2. Animals — Miscellanea — Juvenile literature.
[1. Body size — Miscellanea.   2. Animals — Miscellanea.]   I. Title.
QL799.3.J46   1996
591.4 — dc20   95-41162   CIP   AC

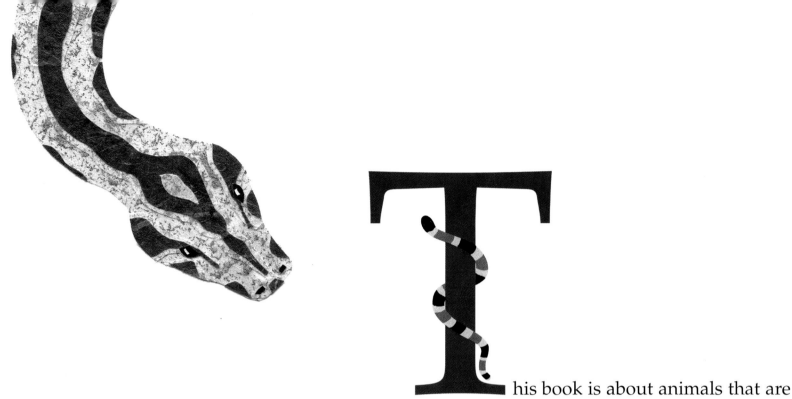

This book is about animals that are related but different in size. How can one bird or snake be so big and another bird or snake be so small?

Related animals of nearly the same size (tigers and leopards, for example) tend to compete for the same places to live and the same food to eat. Through the process of evolution, some animals have become larger or smaller. This has made it easier for them to find food and homes, defend themselves, and hide from their enemies.

All of the creatures in this book are illustrated at the same scale (one inch equals eight inches) so animals throughout the book can be compared. More information about each animal can be found at the back of the book.

When hunting, the Siamese cat acts like its wild cousin, the Siberian tiger.

The ruby-throated hummingbird can fly forward, backward, or straight up and down, but the ostrich can't fly at all.

Both the Nile crocodile and the African chameleon live in tropical Africa.

The capybara, the world's largest rodent, weighs as much as one thousand deer mice.

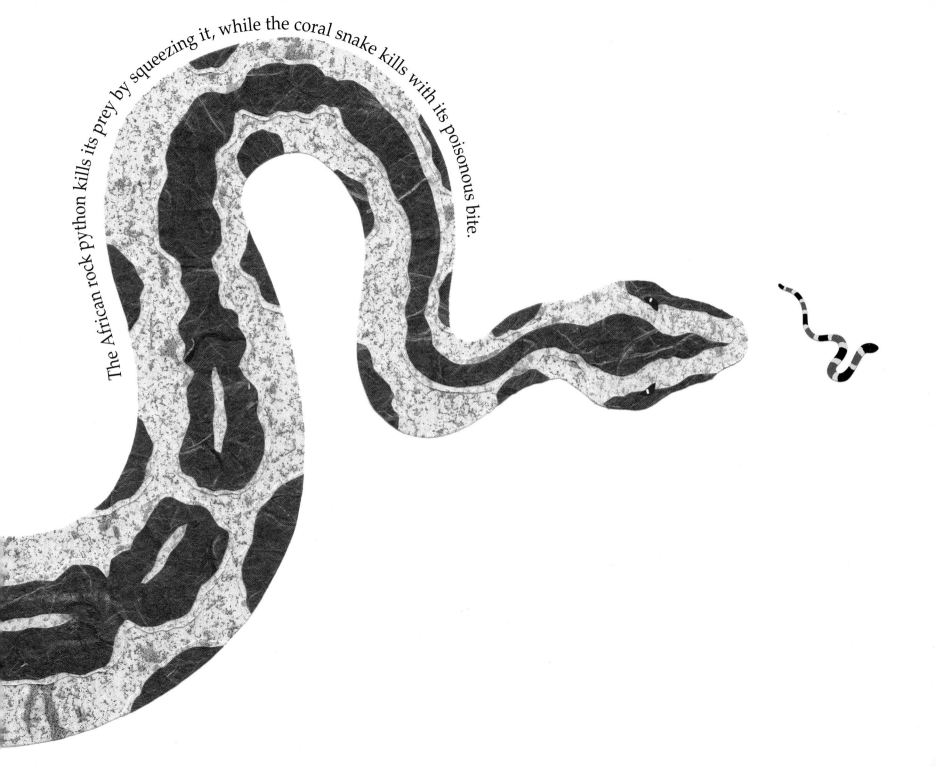

The African rock python kills its prey by squeezing it, while the coral snake kills with its poisonous bite.

A gorilla can weigh as much as four men, while the pygmy marmoset is smaller than a squirrel.

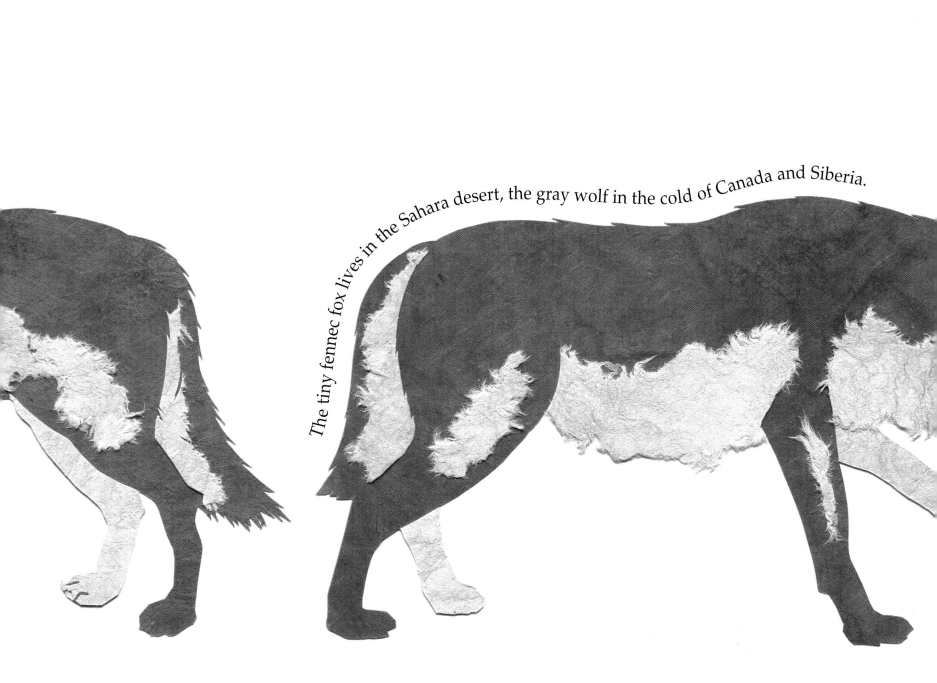

The tiny fennec fox lives in the Sahara desert, the gray wolf in the cold of Canada and Siberia.

The opossum and the red kangaroo are both marsupials—they carry their babies in a pouch.

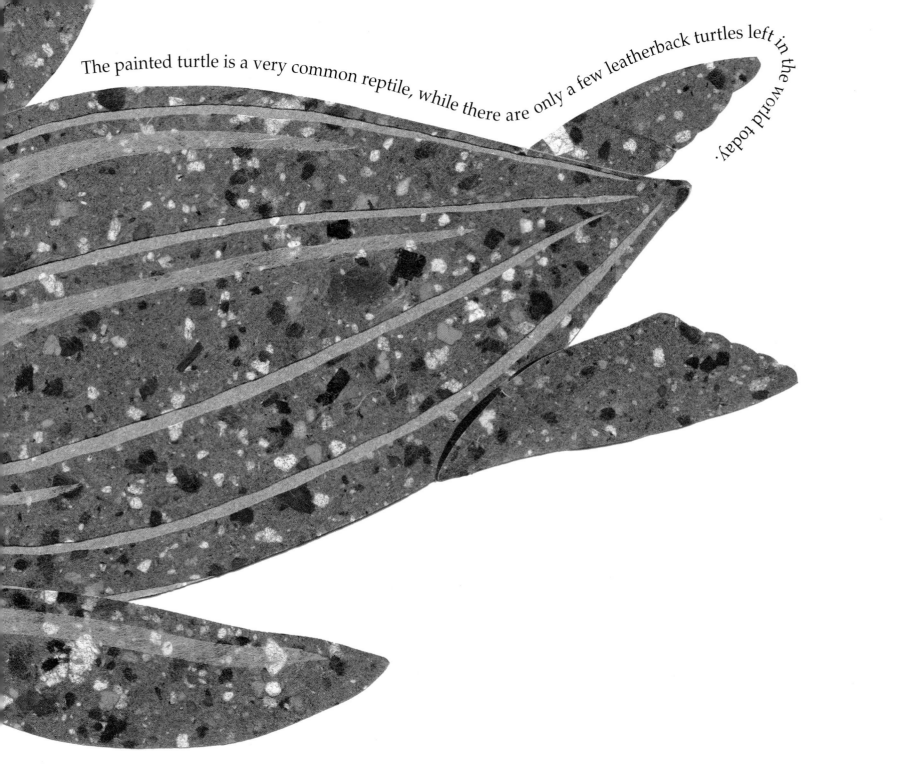

The painted turtle is a very common reptile, while there are only a few leatherback turtles left in the world today.

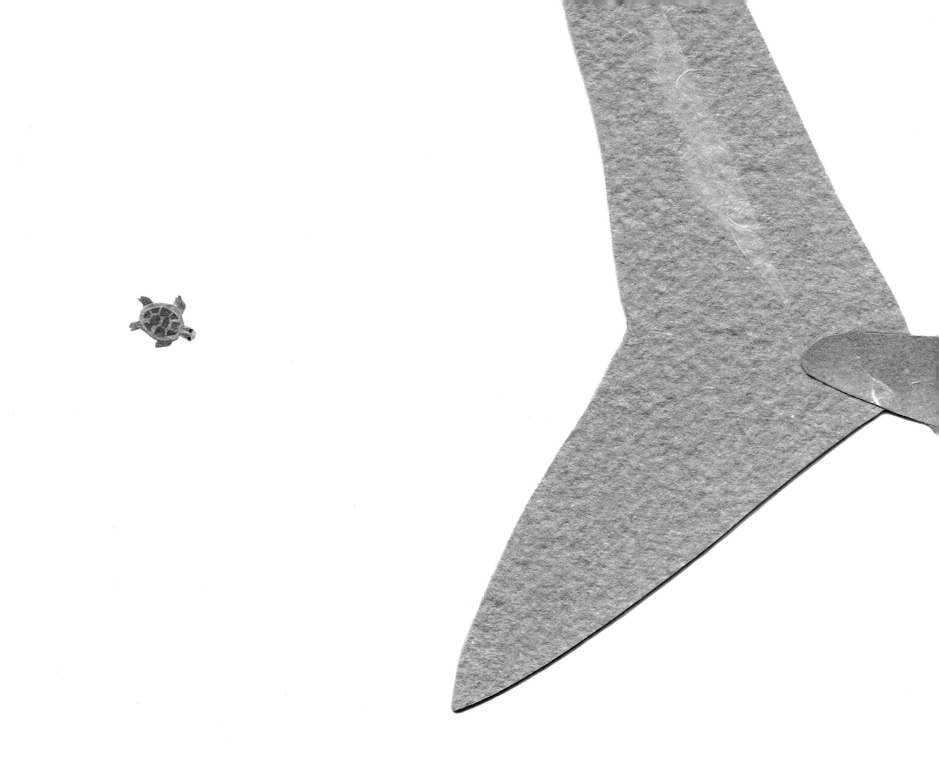

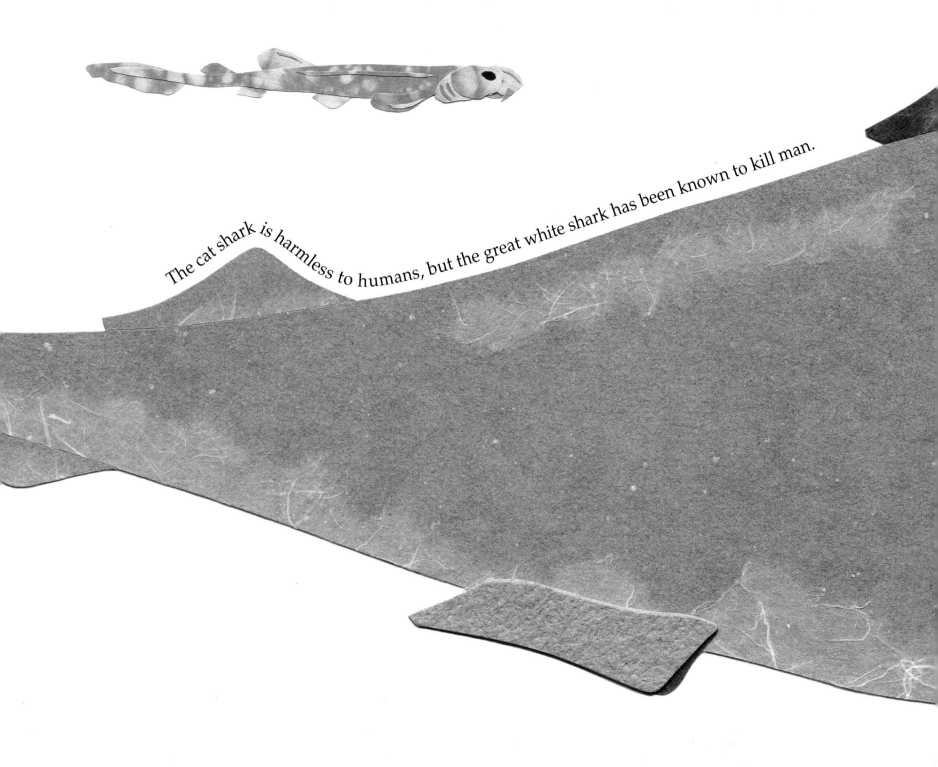

The cat shark is harmless to humans, but the great white shark has been known to kill man.

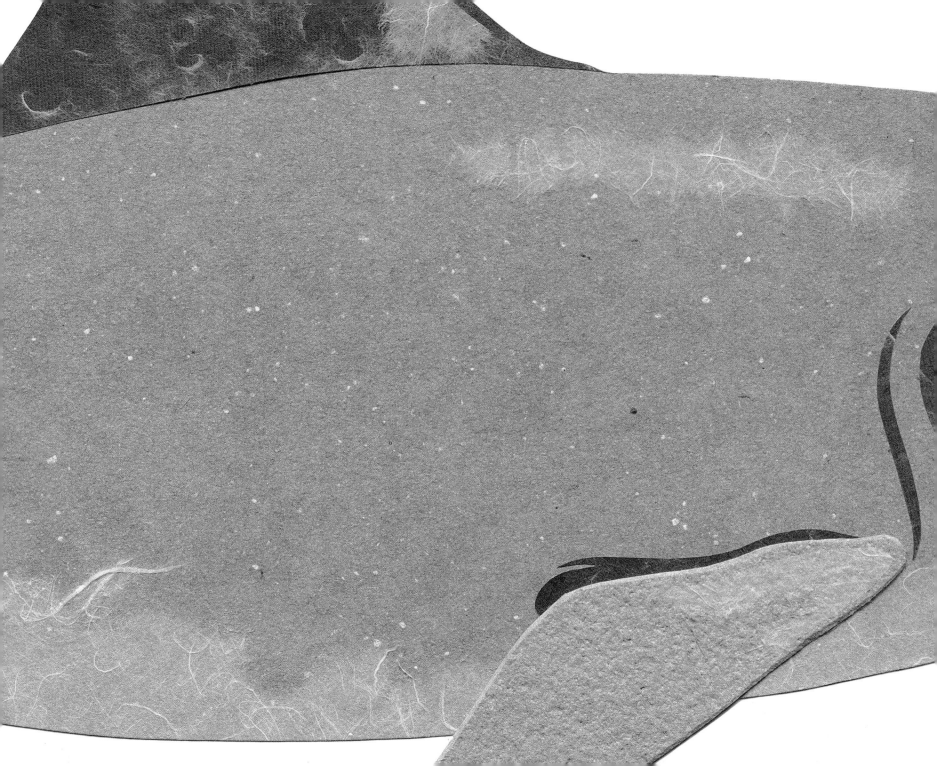

The sea otter weighs about fifty pounds,

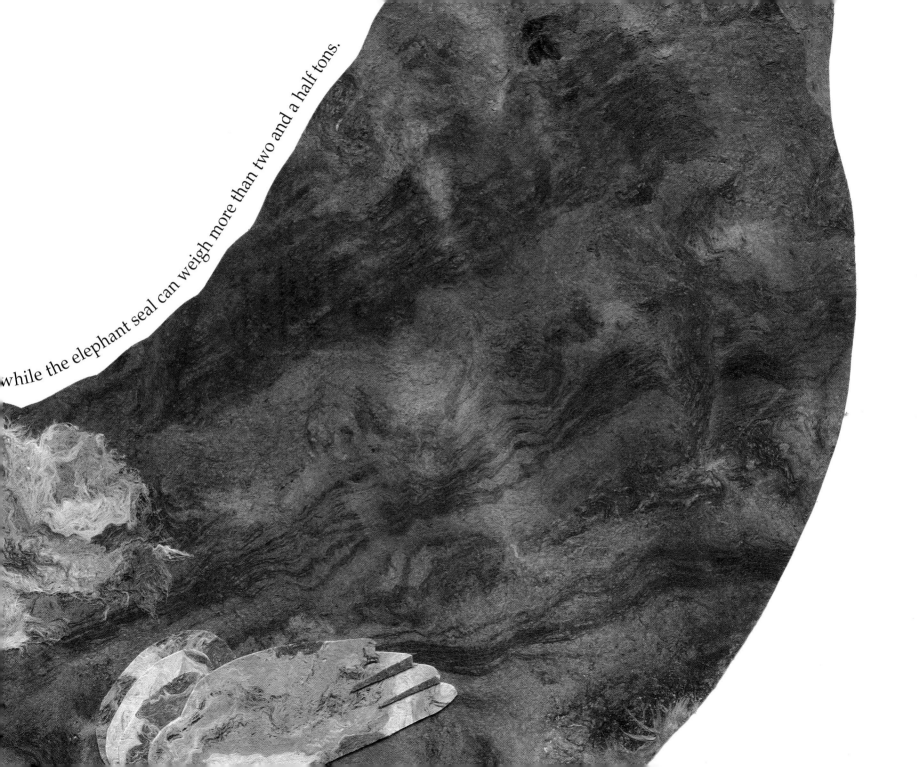

while the elephant seal can weigh more than two and a half tons.

On these pages, animals are shown at the scale of one inch equals two and one-half feet.

Opossum

Red Kangaroo

Siberian Tiger

Ruby-throated
Hummingbird

Ostrich

Siamese Cat

Painted
Turtle

Deer Mouse

Capybara

Cat Shark

Leatherback Turtle

Great White Shark

Coral Snake

African Rock Python

Chameleon

Nile Crocodile

Fennec Fox

Gray Wolf

Pygmy
Marmoset

Elephant
Seal

Gorilla

Sea Otter

Human
Adult

Siberian Tiger

The Siberian tiger can measure 14 feet from the tip of its nose to the tip of its tail and weigh as much as 650 pounds. It lives in northern China and eastern Siberia and eats deer, elk, rabbits, and fish. There are probably only about 200 Siberian tigers left in the wild.

Siamese Cat

One of the smaller house cats, the Siamese cat weighs about 6 pounds and is 18 inches long, including its tail. House cats have been living with people for over 4,000 years, and they usually eat whatever their owners feed them. Many tame cats, though, still like to hunt and will kill and eat birds, mice, frogs, and other small animals.

Ostrich

The largest bird in the world, the ostrich, cannot fly. Ostriches can run very fast, however. Their top speed is around 45 miles per hour — faster than a racehorse! An ostrich can stand over 8 feet tall and weigh as much as 300 pounds. These birds inhabit the grassy plains of Africa.

Ruby-throated Hummingbird

Only 3 inches long and weighing one-half an ounce, this hummingbird lives throughout the eastern United States. It uses its long, slender bill to sip nectar from flowers. Hummingbirds beat their wings up to 60 times a second, so fast that to us they appear as a blur.

Nile Crocodile

This fierce predator is found throughout much of Africa. Up to 20 feet in length and weighing as much as 1,650 pounds, the Nile crocodile eats mammals, reptiles, birds, and fish. It can even eat an animal as large as a buffalo. The crocodile lies in wait in shallow water, and then lunges out to grab its prey and drag it under the surface to drown. Crocodiles can live for more than 100 years.

African Chameleon

The African chameleon is a lizard that has the ability to change its skin color to match its surroundings and hide itself from its enemies. The chameleon is about 12 inches long, and can extend its tongue to nearly 2 times that length. It eats insects and other, smaller lizards.

Capybara

The largest rodent in the world, the capybara is 3 to 4 feet long and can weigh as much as 110 pounds. It lives along rivers in South America and eats the leaves and stems of water plants. The capybara loves to swim and spends much of its time in the water.

Deer Mouse

The deer mouse is found throughout most of North America. From the tip of its nose to the end of its tail, it is about 6 inches long. It eats seeds, nuts, and insects. The deer mouse usually makes its home in underground burrows but sometimes moves into people's homes and builds a nest in a wall or attic.

African Rock Python

This snake grows to 32 feet in length and can weigh 250 pounds. It likes the open country of Africa and eats mammals and birds. The python feeds by squeezing its prey to death and then swallowing it whole. Animals weighing as much as 120 pounds can be eaten in this way. A python doesn't have to eat very often — it can take a whole week to digest one meal.

Coral Snake

This 15-inch-long snake lives in the desert areas of the southwestern United States and Mexico. It eats other snakes and is very poisonous. Its pattern of red, yellow, and black stripes is similar to that of the harmless milk snake, except for the order of the colors. An old rhyme helps us tell one snake from the other: "Red touch black, good for Jack. Red touch yellow, kill a fellow."

Gorilla

The gorilla lives in the lowlands and mountains of central Africa. A peaceful creature who eats bamboo shoots and plant stems, the male gorilla stands over 6 feet tall and can weigh more than 650 pounds. There are only about 450 mountain gorillas left in the world.

Pygmy Marmoset

The smallest of the primates, this South American monkey is only about 6 inches long, with a 7 or 8 inch tail. The pygmy marmoset's hands are too small to grasp most branches, so it climbs trees with its claws, like a squirrel.

Gray Wolf

The gray wolf, 5 feet long and as much as 175 pounds in weight, is found in the northern half of North America, northern Europe, and Asia. It lives and hunts in packs of 7 to 20 wolves. The gray wolf eats deer, elk, rabbits, mice, and even berries, if no other food can be found.

Fennec Fox

The smallest of the foxes, the fennec fox lives in the Sahara Desert in Africa, where it eats rodents and other small animals. Its body is about 10 inches long, and it weighs only 1 1/4 pounds. The Sahara is one of the hottest places on earth, and the fennec fox's large tail and ears help it to get rid of excess heat.

Leatherback Turtle

The leatherback lives in the Pacific Ocean and is larger than any other turtle or tortoise. It can eat poisonous jellyfish without being affected by the stings. This turtle's shell feels leathery, rather than hard. The leatherback is a fast swimmer, and the grooves on its shell help it move easily through the water.

Painted Turtle

One of the most common turtles in North America, the painted turtle lives in ponds and streams and eats water plants, insects, and small fish. It's about 5 inches long, and gets its name from the pattern of bands on its shell and body.

Red Kangaroo

Marsupials are animals who carry and nurse their babies in pouches. The red kangaroo is the largest of the marsupials, standing 6 1/2 feet tall. It lives in Australia and eats grass and other plants. The kangaroo, with its strong back legs, is a great leaper. The red kangaroo can cover over 40 feet in a single jump.

Virginia Opossum

The opossum is the only marsupial that lives in North America. It is about 20 inches long, nose to tail. Newborn opossums are so small at birth that 6 of them could fit in one teaspoon. They spend their early weeks in their mother's pouch. Later they crawl out and cling to the fur on her back. If an opossum feels threatened, it will roll onto its back, let its tongue hang out, and pretend to be dead.

Great White Shark

The great white shark will eat almost any fish or mammal it can catch. It lives in warm and temperate oceans worldwide and usually grows to be 20 to 25 feet long, weighing about 2,500 pounds. The biggest great white shark ever caught was over 36 feet long. No one knows whether sharks sleep, but the great white must swim 24 hours a day to keep water moving over its gills so it can breathe.

Cat Shark

A small member of the shark family, the cat shark is only about 3 feet long. It gets its name from the whisker-like feelers on its face. The cat shark uses these whiskers to help it find the bottom-dwelling animals it eats. This shark isn't dangerous to humans.

Elephant Seal

The southern elephant seal lives on the coast of Antarctica. It eats fish and squid, grows to over 20 feet in length, and weighs as much as 5,000 pounds. Male elephant seals inflate their noses to twice their normal size when they want to impress female seals.

Sea Otter

The sea otter lives in the waters off the West Coast of the United States. Otters are usually about 4 feet long. They eat crabs, sea urchins, and shellfish. An otter sometimes breaks open clams and other shellfish by banging them against a rock which it places on its chest while floating on its back.

Bibliography

Behler, John H., and King, F. Wayne. *The Audubon Society Field Guide to North American Reptiles & Amphibians*, New York: Alfred A. Knopf, 1989.

Burton, Maurice and Robert. *The Encyclopedia of the Animal Kingdom*, New York: Crescent Books, 1976.

Children's Encyclopedia of the Animal Kingdom. Dorset Press, 1992.

Farrand, John, Jr., ed. *The Audubon Society Encyclopedia of Animal Life*, New York: Clarkson N. Potter, 1982.

Mannucci, Maria Pia, and Minelli, Alessandro, ed. *Great Book of the Animal Kingdom*. New York: Arch Cape, 1982.

Robbins, Chandler S.; Brunn, Bertel; and Zim, Herbert S. *Birds of North America*. New York: Golden, 1983.